Dr. D. K. Olukoya

Praying Against The Spirit of THE VALLEY

Warfare Prayer Series **14**

Praying Against The Spirit of The Valley

DR. D. K. OLUKOYA

D. K. OLUKOYA

PRAYING AGAINST THE SPIRIT OF THE VALLEY
© 2005 DR. D. K. OLUKOYA
ISBN-978-38083-5-4
1st Printing - May 2005 AD

Published by:

The Battle Cry Christian Ministries

322, Herbert Macaulay Street, Sabo, Yaba, P. O. Box 12272,
Ikeja, Lagos.

Phone: 0803-304-4239, 01-8044415

FOREIGN CORRESPONDENCES
UNITED STATES
Phone: 404-454-3358

GHANA
Phone: 24236113

All Scripture quotations are from the King James Version of the Bible

Cover illustration: Sister Shade Olukoya
All rights reserved.
We prohibit reproduction in whole or part without written permission.

TABLE OF CONTENTS

1. PRAYING AGAINST THE VALLEY SPIRIT ...... -4-

2. POWER AGAINST BAG WITH HOLES .... -25-

3. DEALING WITH SPIRITUAL BARRIERS .... -37-

D. K. OLUKOYA

CHAPTER 1
PRAYING AGAINST THE VALLEY SPIRIT

PRAYING AGAINST THE SPIRIT OF THE VALLEY

The phenomenon of the valley spirit has remained veiled to many believers and Christian leaders alike. Many are completely ignorant of the valley spirit and this has kept many people in darkness. They have known no victory and life has not been palatable to them. If you do not know what the valley spirit means it is possible for you to remain at the dunghill for the rest of your life. That is why you must pray against this wicked spirit.

You can overcome and you will overcome in the name of Jesus. It goes without saying that ignorance is a disease and knowledge is power. It is ignorance that makes you become enslaved to the control of valley spirits. But knowledge will arm you with all the tools needed to experience resounding victory. This book will show you the weapons of warfare, which you must make use of before victory can come your way.

THE SPIRIT OF THE VALLEY

You may ask, "What is the valley spirit?" Valley spirit is the spirit of the tail or the spirit of failure. This spirit has reduced giants to dwarves spiritually, academically and in other areas of life. The valley spirit carries out its operations at the bottom region. This spirit brings people down from the level of stardom to the dust. Also, many celebrities have been reduced to wrecks through the operation of this wicked spirit.

The valley spirit will never allow you to be triumphant in life. People that are troubled by the valley spirit do not live up to expectations. It is these kind of people, who give up easily or get discouraged. When you overcome the spirit of the valley the sky will no more be your limit. In fact, at old age, your strength will remain like that of a youth. You will also break jinxes and never break down.

God remains the strength of your life. Caleb overcame the valley spirit through the confession of faith. Joshua overcame and he told the children of Israel that they could get to the Promised Land. In fact, at the age of 85, Caleb was still invigorated to fight the battles of the Lord. Read this account.

Joshua 14:6-15: Then the children of Judah came unto Joshua in Gilgal: and Caleb the son of Jephunneh the Kenezite said unto him, Thou knowest the thing that the Lord said unto Moses the man of God concerning me and thee in Kadesh-barnea. Forty years old was I when Moses the servant of the Lord sent me from

PRAYING AGAINST THE SPIRIT OF THE VALLEY

Kadesh-barnea to espy out the land; and I brought him word again as it was in mine heart. Nevertheless my brethren that went up with me made the heart of the people melt: but I wholly followed the Lord my God. And Moses sware on that day, saying, Surely the land whereon thy feet have trodden shall be thine inheritance, and thy children's for ever, because thou hast wholly followed the Lord my God. And now, behold, the Lord hath kept me alive, as he said, these forty and five years, even since the Lord spake this word unto Moses, while the children of Israel wandered in the wilderness: and now, lo, I am this day fourscore and five years old. As yet I am as strong this day as I was in the day that Moses sent me: as my strength was then, even so is my strength now, for war, both to go out, and to come in. Now therefore give me this mountain, whereof the Lord spake in that day; for thou heardest in that day how the Anakims were there, and that the cities were great and fenced: if so be the Lord will be with me, then I shall be able to drive them out, as the Lord said. And Joshua blessed him, and gave unto Caleb the son of Jephunneh Hebron for an inheritance. Hebron therefore became the inheritance of Caleb the son of Jephunneh the Kenezite unto this day, because that he wholly followed the Lord God of Israel. And the name of Hebron before was Kirjath-arba; which Arba was a great man among the Anakims. And the land had rest from war.

THE SET TIME

This is the set time for you to leave the lowly valley and get to the mountaintop. The valley is not meant for the Children of God. It is on the mountaintop that God expects you to be. The God you serve does not dwell in the valley, and you cannot afford to be labelled as a valley dweller. You can leave the valley and get to the zenith. God wants to position you at the top. What you need to do is to lift up your heart and your hands so that God can take you up.

Enough is enough. It is the will of God for your life to blossom at the top. Do you know that God wants you to ride upon the high places of the earth? The Bible says: "If thou turn away thy foot from the sabbath, from doing thy pleasure on my holy day; and call the sabbath a delight, the holy of the LORD, honourable; and shalt honour him, not doing thine own ways, nor finding thine own pleasure, nor speaking thine own words: Then shalt thou delight thyself in the LORD; and I will cause thee to ride upon the high places of the earth, and feed thee with the heritage of Jacob thy father: for the mouth of the LORD hath spoken it" Isa 58:13-14.

Now is the time for you to depart from the low land and the valley. Your feet must be set on high places.

PRAYING AGAINST THE SPIRIT OF THE VALLEY

NO SECOND PLACE

Do you know that God has only one place for everyone? God did not provide a second alternative for you. The will and the purpose of God for you is the best and the first class in life. Never settle for the second class in life.

There is something unfortunate about many people on the face of the earth. It is the fact that almost the entire humanity accepts the second place in life. This may surprise you. It is a fact that you need to know. In fact, I don't know if you are one of those inhabitants of the earth who have settled for the second best in life. It is either that you are in God's position for you or not; there are no two ways about it. You cannot be on the fence as far as God's positioning is concerned.

A SURPRISE

Let me be honest with you, and this may be a surprise to you, but I need to reveal it.

The average man develops ten per cent of his talents. This revelation should put you on your feet and make you rise up to the challenge of maximizing your full potentials.

Paul, the apostle was sufficiently aware of this phenomenon and that made him not be satisfied with any level in which he found himself. His earnest prayer is "Lord, take me to a higher ground." He was dissatisfied with his spiritual level.

Does that baffle you? Paul had wonderful experiences with the Lord. In fact, there was a time he got to the third heavens, where he heard unspeakable words which human minds cannot fathom. Paul had raised the dead and performed many miracles. To human judgment, Paul was a symbol of perfection, to the extent that God gave him diverse spiritual gifts. He was mightily used to proclaim the gospel among the gentiles. Paul could be called a radical preacher of the gospel. In fact, Paul accomplished more for the gospel than all the other apostles who were with Christ when he was on earth. This same Paul the apostle had this to say:

Philip. 3:13-14: Brethren, I count not myself to have apprehended: but this one thing I do, forgetting those things which are behind, and reaching forth unto those things which are before, I press toward the mark for the prize of the high calling of God in Christ Jesus.

Dissatisfaction with your present state is a great weapon to fight the spirit of the valley. It is until you come to terms with the devastating effects of the valley spirit that you can pray aggressively and triumph over against the spirit of the valley.

THE PLAN

Jesus came to the scene to put an end to this evil trend in man's life. He has the key to unlock you from the valley of failure, fear, disappointment and death. He says in John 10:10: "The thief cometh not, but for to steal, and to kill, and to destroy: I am come that they might have life, and that they might have it more abundantly.

You will discover that the valley spirit is a thief and has come to steal, kill and destroy. But there is hope because when Jesus Christ came to the stage, he brought abundant life. Abundant life is life in all its fullness. It is life at the top and not in the valley. The life is abundant in all sense of the word. This is the plan of God. God wants you to have life more abundantly and not manage to eke out an existence. Anything less than abundant life is the valley spirit and you have to reject it by fire.

It is disastrous for a child of God to settle for anything

below excellence. It is tragic for a child of a king to settle for the dust-bin when he is supposed to dine with the God of heaven and earth.

When you have victory over the valley, you will never be turned to a second-class citizen. Don't allow the enemy to make you give up.

The giants in the realm of your mountain will become bread for you when you leave the valley to confront them on the mountain.

NEVER SETTLE FOR LESS

A child of God who has conquered the valley spirit will never settle for less in life. Your focus and desire should be God's best. God's best can never be anything less than the best. You need to re-orientate yourself and rekindle the fire of breakthroughs and the best into your spirit. The thoughts of God are higher than our thoughts. That is why we cannot afford to grope in darkness when the Almighty has prepared to take us to the top of the mountain.

Isaiah 55:8-11: For my thoughts are not your thoughts, neither are your ways my ways, saith the Lord. For as the heavens are higher than the earth, so are my ways higher than your ways, and

PRAYING AGAINST THE SPIRIT OF THE VALLEY

my thoughts than your thoughts. For as the rain cometh down, and the snow from heaven, and returneth not thither, but watereth the earth, and maketh it bring forth and bud, that it may give seed to the sower, and bread to the eater: So shall my word be that goeth forth out of my mouth: it shall not return unto me void, but it shall accomplish that which I please, and it shall prosper in the thing whereto I sent it.

Never must it be heard that you are looking down on yourself. You are a gem in this world. There is a sleeping giant lying within you. Don't relegate yourself to the level of a grasshopper. Tell your soul and spirit that you are not meant for the bottom. And you cannot settle for less. Wake up from your slumber!

You have not reached the level God wants you to be. You have to break loose from the grip of the valley spirit. You are meant for the mountain top.

THE CONTRAST

A lot of people do not possess the spirit of Caleb. It is rare to find the spirit of Caleb in the lives of many people today. So many people are embracing mediocrity. They are busy signing peace agreement with the spirit of the valley. Who told you to be satisfied with your spiritual level? What gives you the impression that you have attained God's best for your life and ministry? Do you know that your maximum is God's minimum? In fact, your best is God's stating point. Get ready for a divine lifting. God will catapult you to the mountain that is greater than you.

A LOOSER? NO!

Anyone that sticks to the low land will always remain a looser. That is why you should detest being on the low land. You become a winner when you defeat the valley spirit. You must not be divinely satisfied with the valley, aimed at the higher ground. This has to be done because God has better things for you. Being at the valley will make you to be blind to the great things that God has prepared for you at the top.

NEVER TO BE HEALED

The valley spirit makes its victim a looser. It can imprison anyone who fails to take a decisive step.

Prayer warriors once prayed for the healing of a sister who had been on sick bed for a long time, but nothing happened. They prayed time and again but answers remained elusive.

The Holy Spirit later spoke to one of the prayer warriors that they should ask the sister if she really wanted to be healed. It appeared foolish, but one of the prayer warriors asked the question. They were surprised at the response which they got from her. She stated that she did not want to be healed. By the time the prayer warrior asked her her reason for not wanting healing, she said that when she was healthy, her husband was not always at home. It is only when she is sick that her husband would stay around her at home. She maintained that if the only reason the man would come home was for her to be sick, then she would not like to be healed. She wanted the man to stay around her. But the valley spirit later caught up with the life of the sister. Seven days later she died. Her husband eventually married another wife after her demise. This is a kind of havoc that the valley spirit can do in the life of anyone.

FACTS OF LIFE

An employee must not remain an employee forever. If you are destined to own a bank, do not remain as account clerk forever.

A person under control should aspire to become a controller, and a servant must aspire to be a boss.

A man should not be a chief tenant forever, but he should aspire to be a landlord.

A dwarf should aspire to become a giant. That is why you need to ask for the anointing to excel in anything you lay your hands upon. You have to prove to the world that the hosts of heaven are backing you.

You must wake up from spiritual slumber and put on your battle armour. Aggressive prayer must be directed to challenge the giants that are occupying the mountains of your life. Why must you remain poor when the wealth of God has been made available for you.

THE ROAD TO THE PROMISED LAND

Heaven is not meant for those who doubt the power of God. In fact, without faith it is impossible to please God. God has a promised land for you. Faith in God combined with courage will make you to overcome the valley spirit. You must place your trust in Him. Do you know that you have to overcome the valley spirit before you can put your

PRAYING AGAINST THE SPIRIT OF THE VALLEY

feet on the promised land? The children of Israel and the elders that were sent to go and spy the promised land allowed the spirit of the valley to overcome them and so they missed out on the promise of God.

Pay attention to this point. The Amalekites and the Cannanites, whom the Israelites were afraid of had a covenant with the valley spirit. In fact, the Scripture makes it clear that the people dwelt in the valley. Caleb never allowed the influence of the valley spirit to affect him and he received God's commendation.

Numbers 14:24-25: But my servant Caleb, because he had another spirit with him, and hath followed me fully, him will I bring into the land whereinto he went; and his seed shall possess it. (Now the Amalekites and the Canaanites dwelt in the valley.) To morrow turn you, and get you into the wilderness by the way of the Red sea.

Caleb and Joshua got to the promised land because they overcame the valley spirit. Almost all the children of Israel got lost because they yielded to the valley spirit. The valley spirit which operated at the valley of Eschol discouraged their hearts and this made the anger of the Lord to be kindled upon them.

Numbers 32:9-14: For when they went up unto the valley of

Eshcol, and saw the land, they discouraged the heart of the children of Israel, that they should not go into the land which the Lord had given them. And the Lord's anger was kindled the same time, and he sware, saying, Surely none of the men that came up out of Egypt, from twenty years old and upward, shall see the land which I sware unto Abraham, unto Isaac, and unto Jacob; because they have not wholly followed me: Save Caleb the son of Jephunneh the Kenezite, and Joshua the son of Nun: for they have wholly followed the Lord. And the Lord's anger was kindled against Israel, and he made them wander in the wilderness forty years, until all the generation, that had done evil in the sight of the Lord, was consumed. And, behold, ye are risen up in your fathers' stead, an increase of sinful men, to augment yet the fierce anger of the Lord toward Israel.

You must not allow the valley spirit to discourage you on the road to heaven. God can make you a conqueror and an overcomer.

PRAYERS AGAINST THE VALLEY SPIRIT

Prayer is the master key through which you can war against the valley spirit. At this point I will give you the kind of prayers that can cripple and destroy the valley spirit.

☞ PRAY TO DETERMINE YOUR MOUNTAIN

This kind of prayer is tantamount to knowing where your

PRAYING AGAINST THE SPIRIT OF THE VALLEY

goals and destiny lie. It is until you locate the mountain where God expects you to be that you can have a change for better in life. Without focus, you fail as far as warfare prayer is concerned. Envision on the mountain that God wants you to be.

The mountain that God wants you to be is the height that God wants you to reach in life. Caleb had a target and a goal. By the time he met Joshua, he did not waste time in making his request. He told Joshua to give him mount Hebron and he got it.

Joshua 14:12-13: Now therefore give me this mountain, whereof the Lord spake in that day; for thou heardest in that day how the Anakims were there, and that the cities were great and fenced: if so be the Lord will be with me, then I shall be able to drive them out, as the Lord said. And Joshua blessed him, and gave unto Caleb the son of Jephunneh Hebron for an inheritance.

If you don't know your goals, you wouldn't know what to pursue; and if you don't know what you are after, you won't be able to pray effectively. You cannot find something until you define it.

The account of blind Bartimeus captures vividly what it means to pray with determination, against the valley spirit. He heard that Jesus Christ was passing by and demonstrated readiness to break lose from the valley spirit, which kept him in blindness. His determination to obtain deliverance made him to cry to Jesus with persistence, despite the fact that people tried to silence him. Jesus stopped and asked him what he wanted. Without beating about the bush, he said, "That I may receive my sight". And because of his faith and focus, his request was granted.

Mark 14:46-52: And they laid their hands on him, and took him. And one of them that stood by drew a sword, and smote a servant of the high priest, and cut off his ear. And Jesus answered and said unto them, Are ye come out, as against a thief, with swords and with staves to take me? I was daily with you in the temple teaching, and ye took me not: but the scriptures must be fulfilled. And they all forsook him, and fled. And there followed him a certain young man, having a linen cloth cast about his naked body; and the young men laid hold on him: And he left the linen cloth, and fled from them naked.

Do not settle for mediocrity because you may end up a mediocre. Do not grab anything that comes your way, because you may grab the shadow and miss the real thing when it comes. Cultivate the habit of praying to find out where you are supposed to be. The deliverance from valley spirit begins when you pray to know where you were made to be in God's plan.

PRAYING AGAINST THE SPIRIT OF THE VALLEY

☞ PRAY TO PURSUE YOUR HIGHER GROUND

After you must have prayed to discover your goals and mountains, you will take another bold step of faith to pray in order to discover your higher ground.

I had a revelation while I was praying for a brother many years ago. The brother was very intelligent, but things were not working for him. In that revelation I saw the brother climbing a staircase of about 14 steps; He was on the 3rd step. I also saw a red mark on the 10th step to signify that that was where he was supposed to be. Then I saw a naked woman holding his right leg and he was struggling to break loose from the grip of the woman. I told the brother what I saw, and I asked him to tell me who the woman was. He told me that it must be the woman, whom he wanted to marry, but eventually he did not marry her. He said that the woman threatened to deal with him.

Caleb and blind Bartimeus pursued their mountains and goals rigorously before they could get their hearts desire. Caleb's desire was to take the mountain while Bartimeus' was to regain his sight.

Your birthright - Do you know that failure is not from

God but from the devil? Failure is associated with the valley spirit. You should never be known for failure. Success is your birthright as a born again child of God. It is your redemptive right and your heritage.

You have no excuse if you fail. Christians should be the best in their field of endeavors. Christian students should be the best; they should be ten times better than their colleagues. It is a shame for a believer to fail examinations or to repeat classes or carry over some courses. Why? It is because you are at an advantage in all ramifications. You have the Holy Ghost (the best teacher) who can teach you all things including your academics. If you are a child of God, you should not be distracted by sin. You can pray and make use of heaven's resources. That is why you cannot fail.

Pray for spiritual discipline. For you to be victorious, and overcome, you need to be disciplined. It is discipline that will make you to be the kind of person that God wants you to be. There is a level of discipline required of you to be able to reach a particular goal in life. If the enemy has destroyed your spiritual discipline, you need to pray to have it restored.

PRAYING AGAINST THE SPIRIT OF THE VALLEY

☞ PRAY FOR DILIGENCE AND DETERMINATION

Lack of diligence and determination will make you to fall short of the glory of God. Diligence and determination will make you to overcome the spirit of the valley. This kind of quality will help you to overcome the spirit of the valley.

☞ PRAY TO DRIVE OUT TRESPASSERS AWAY FROM YOUR MOUNTAIN

This is the kind of Prayer that must be directed at driving away giants that want to occupy your mountain. There is a need for you to exercise faith and courage before you can rise to the mountain top. Wage war against spiritual giants who seem to be obstinate or stubborn.

PRAYER POINTS

1. Stubborn bewitchment, what are you waiting for? Die in Jesus' name.

2. Every witchcraft giant of poverty, die today, in the name of Jesus.

3. Thou power of marriage destruction, die in the name of Jesus.

4. Every arrow of witchcraft, fired into my dream, backfire, today in the name of Jesus.

5. Every arrow of infirmity and untimely death, go back to your sender in the name of Jesus.

6. Every cage of witchcraft, release my star in the name of Jesus.

7. Oh Lord! Ordain terrifying noise against the enemies of my breakthrough in the name of Jesus.

8. Oh God that answers by fire, answer my request and I shall glorify your name.

9. Oh thou that troubleth my Israel, my God shall trouble you today in the name of Jesus.

CHAPTER 2
POWER AGAINST BAG WITH HOLES

Financial success has remained elusive to many people because of bags with a hole. There are many people today who cannot lay claim to one or two achievements throughout their life long labour. So many are struggling with the yoke of poverty because of bags with holes. Bags with holes can reduce a prosperous man to a pauper. That is why you need to examine yourself to know whether a bag with holes is in operation in your life.

I want you to pray aggressively in order to deal decisively with the bag with holes. The following prayer points will change your status.

PRAYER POINTS

1. Internal witchcraft arrows, die in the name of Jesus.

2. I shall arise and depart from every evil pattern in the name of Jesus

3. The mouth of the wicked speaking against me shall speak no more in the name of Jesus.

4. This year I forbid you to record any problem against me in the name of Jesus.

PRAYING AGAINST THE SPIRIT OF THE VALLEY

5. Fire of God arise and destroy my stubborn problems in the name of Jesus

6. Let the glory of my Pharaoh die in the name of Jesus.

7. My glory shall not die in the name of Jesus

8. Every power stealing from me in the dream what are you waiting for? Die in the name of Jesus.

Prophet Haggai gave a clear description of the spiritual bag with holes. The Bible says;

Haggai 1:6: Ye have sown much, and bring in little; ye eat, but ye have not enough; ye drink, but ye are not filled with drink; ye clothe you, but there is none warm; and he that earneth wages earneth wages to put it into a bag with holes.

The bag described above does not in any way mean a physical bag, but it refers to a bag in the spiritual realm. This spiritual bag stores the blessings of many people. The problem of many people today is not that they do not attend prayer meetings, but their bag is leaking. This spiritual leakage always brings their efforts to the realm of non-achievement.

What you will discover is that many people generally approach the river of life with buckets full of holes. The enemy has stolen buckets without holes and has replaced them with perforated ones. God cannot pour His avalanche of blessings into a bucket full of holes. Until such spiritual holes are sealed, a person with a bag with holes will lose out on God's blessings. In fact, such a person can be likened to a fisherman who caught a fish with the hook he has. Moreover the only worm he could catch has been taken away by the fish, which escaped into the river after being caught.

AN EXAMPLE

Maybe you want to know what exactly is meant by the term "bag with holes." A good example is what happened to a sister. The sister signed an agreement with a pharmaceutical shop she wanted to work with. She agreed that in the course of any loss in the shop she would be liable to settle the payment of all lost items. So before she collects her salary, the stock of all the drugs in the store has to be taken, so that if there is any loss, the cost of such thing will be deducted from her salary. At the end of a particular month, drugs worth ₦15,000:00 were stolen and her salary was ₦5,000:00. This gives us a good example of a bag with holes. You need to pray against this evil phenomenon.

A person with a leaking financial bag would earn so much, but would not be able to account for it. He cannot sit back and tell how he spends the money. This reminds me of somebody that I prayed with some years ago. In July he had made up to 16 million Naira, but by December he had only ₦6,500:00 in his account. The problem with him was the phenomenon of the bag with holes.

If you notice in your life that you are a workaholic and yet you only have little gain, you have the problem with a leaking bag. When you discover that you are the first person to arrive at your place of work and you close late without any visible achievement, that means you have to pray against bags with holes.

BEFORE YOU PRAY

I want to state, at his point that you need to examine yourself, you may need to pay your tithes correctly. If you do not pay your tithes and offerings, it is God Himself who will puncture your financial bag, and you know you cannot pray against God. The Bible says;

Malachi 3:8-12: Will a man rob God? Yet ye have robbed me. But ye say, Wherein have we robbed thee? In tithes and offerings. Ye are cursed with a curse: for ye have robbed me, even this whole nation. Bring ye all the tithes into the storehouse, that there may be meat in mine house, and prove me now herewith, saith the Lord of hosts, if I will not open you the windows of heaven, and pour you out a blessing, that there shall not be room enough to receive it. And I will rebuke the devourer for your sakes, and he shall not destroy the fruits of your ground; neither shall your vine cast her fruit before the time in the field, saith the Lord of hosts. And all nations shall call you blessed: for ye shall be a delightsome land, saith the Lord of hosts.

It is when you have settled the problem of tithes and offerings that you can pray the following prayers.

1. Every power constructing bags with holes for me, die in Jesus' name.

2. I command the bag with holes to be sealed by the blood of Jesus in Jesus' name.

3. Let there be an exchange of the bag with holes with the one without holes in the name of Jesus.

HOW TO RECOGNISE BAGS WITH HOLES

If you notice that you easily lose your job, you have to pray against bags with holes. It is the power of bags with holes that disallows customers and clients from patronizing you. The agents of demotion that have been assigned to follow you on your path to success will give way to angelic advancement that will hasten your prosperity. But this can only be possible through prayers.

You can also discover bags with holes when your customers begin to look for somewhere else to buy the same goods which you sell. If you discover that any time you make big profit there would always be a corresponding big problem that will swallow it, you have to pray against the bag with holes. When you discover that debts surround you like the sea, then you have a bag with holes.

If you have unexplainable loss of money or your health is problematic, you need to incapacitate the bag with holes. When you are always duped, there is a bag with holes somewhere. Being financially handicapped despite reasonable income is an evidence of a bag with holes.

YOUR SPIRITUAL LIFE BAG

From the foregoing, you will discover that I have taken time to explain bags with holes in the area of finance.

I want to state clearly here that it is possible to have bags with holes in the spiritual realm. In other words, your spiritual life could be leaking. Your prayer should be that the spiritual leakages be blocked.

HOW TO IDENTIFY SPIRITUAL LEAKAGE

If you live on past glories, your spiritual life is leaking. People who say "once upon a time, I was this and that" have lost the touch of heaven because their bags are leaking spiritually. If you were speaking in tongues before and now you are no more speaking, your spiritual bag is leaking. Maybe, you are used to seeing vision and prophesying in the past, but the story is not the same now, the bag of your spiritual life has been replaced with bags with holes.

In those days you never boarded a public bus without preaching, but the reverse is the case today. Now you are lukewarm and terrible dreams have taken over your sleep. That is an indication of the fact that you have a spiritual bag with holes.

THE ATTITUDE

You cannot afford to fold your hands and allow your spiritual life to degenerate. What you need to do is to pray so that the evil bag will be taken away from you and that the power of God should fill you on a daily basis. You should also clear away the enemy hindering you from regaining your resources. The power that also wastes resources should die in your life. Another attitude of prayer which you need to put forth is that the fresh fire of the Holy Ghost should fill your life from the crown of your head to the sole of your feet.

YOUR PHYSICAL LIFE BAG

The third bag that could leak is the bag of your physical life. When you notice constant failure in examinations and lateness to important meetings, the bag of physical life leaking. Your physical bag may be leaking when you experience constant memory failure. Another way to know that your physical life bag is leaking is that when you cannot hold good things for a long time. If you find opportunities slipping off your hands you have a problem. Serious prayers will have to be offered. When you don't have a settled home, and you quarrel every day to drive away good things from your home, you must pray. Serious prayer has to be made when you are always provoked out of position when you are at the point of your breakthrough.

DREAMS THAT SYPHON BLESSINGS

Certain dreams will reveal to you that your blessings are siphoned. For instance you may have had a dream in which people forcefully collected something from you. Such a dream is an indication of the presence of spiritual leakage. When you have a dream in which you find yourself lavishing money on people, you have to pray. Seeing yourself in a dream buying things you need and things you do not need are an indication that you have to pray against the spirit that siphons your blessings.

If you see your pocket empty and you are counting coins in the dream, you have to pray. If you see you properties being auctioned in the dream, you have to intensify your prayers. When you endlessly search for something in the dream without finding it, you have to go down on your

PRAYING AGAINST THE SPIRIT OF THE VALLEY

knees for serious prayers.

It could even be that you are climbing a stair case without getting to the end of it. When you are supposed to pluck good fruits from a big tree, but you see yourself plucking the unripe ones, you need to pray aggressive prayers. You need to pray aggressively when someone is injecting you in the dream with a syringe. All these are pointers to strategies that the devil use to siphon blessings away from somebody.

Another way satanic operation can be revealed is when you dream seeing yourself being buried or seeing your name among the candidates enlisted for failure. When there is a bag with holes in your life, two spirits come into operation.

- The spirit of frustration
- The spirit of discouragement

The set time for your deliverance has come. God will deliver you from the grip of powers that is producing bags with holes into your life. As you go through the prayer points below God will replace a bag with holes with bags of prosperity, in Jesus' name.

PRAYER POINTS

1. Every robber of my destiny, die in the name of Jesus.

2. I command my spirit to drop every bag with a hole, in Jesus' name.

3. Holy Ghost and fire, possess my possessions for me, in the name of Jesus.

CHAPTER 3
DEALING WITH SPIRITUAL BARRIERS

The subject of spiritual barriers cannot be overemphasized. It plays a crucial role as far as your breakthroughs and blessings are concerned. Ignorance of spiritual barriers will do more harm than good in your life. A spiritual barrier is a potent weapon in the hands of the devil through which he torments bonafide children of God's kingdom. The spiritual barrier is tantamount to satanic bondage. It is only when you are able to understand the concept of spiritual barriers that you can lay claim to being victorious over satanic bondages.

To get started, take the following prayer points

PRAYER POINTS

1. Every foundational power working against my complete deliverance, die in Jesus' name.

2. Every power of my father's house contesting for my deliverance, die in the name of Jesus.

3. Every power of my family line, arguing with my angel of breakthroughs, die in the name of Jesus.

4. Every arrow of the enemy fired into my head, backfire,

PRAYING AGAINST THE SPIRIT OF THE VALLEY

in the name of Jesus.

The number of years you will spend in Satan's territory and dominion lies squarely on the time you are able to discover and destroy your spiritual barriers.

Do you know that the problem in your life and family lingers because of the evil influence of satanic barriers? So many believers are denied of enjoying the liberty, which Christ has purchased because of the barriers, which the devil has placed on the way to deliverance.

Against this backdrop, efforts will be channelled to unveiling the mystery behind spiritual barriers. In this chapter you will also have insight into what spiritual barriers mean. We shall examine this topic with practical application of scriptures and relevant allusions to life experiences. You will never remain the same by the time you are through with this chapter.

Spiritual barriers will be better understood when we pay attention to the associates of barriers. Spiritual barriers can operate in different forms and shades. Let's examine some of the ways barriers can come into operation.

SPIRITUAL BARRIERS AND HINDRANCES

A barrier is akin to hindrance. For you to understand the issue of a spiritual barrier, you need to have knowledge of satanic hindrances. It should be clear to you that the devil has hindered so many people from fulfilling God's purpose for their lives through the manipulation of spiritual barriers. That is why you need to pray aggressively so that all hindrances on your way will give way for harvests of supernatural blessings.

BARRIER AND BONDAGE

To be enslaved under satanic bondage is a product of a spiritual barrier. You cannot boast of breaking barriers without breaking bondage. In fact, to be under bondage is to be a slave to barriers to breakthroughs. Attention must be given to dealing a devastating blow on the bondage before you can say that you are victorious over barriers.

LIMITED BY BARRIERS

Another form of a satanic barrier is limitation. To be limited is to be under a particular barrier. It is only when you have victory over limitation that you can move forward and get your potentials fully realized. Limitation has made many people to be self-satisfied with the average position. Limitation is the arch-enemy of progress and successful achievement.

IMPRISONED BY BARRIERS

Do you know that barriers will imprison its captives? The grip of barriers over the lives of people is not tolerable at all. Being under a barrier is to be limited to the four-walls of the satanic prison. When this happens, all hopes become lost and there seems to be darkness everywhere. It is the power of God that can set you totally free from the imprisonment of the devil.

A barrier is also an obstacle preventing someone from moving from one position to a better position. It limits movement, progress and achievements. A barrier can also be likened to a veil, which covers one from seeing God's divine purpose and destiny. You can also look at a barrier as a wicked arrangement designed to keep a person stationary. It is the presence of a barrier that makes you beat about the bush without hitting the nail on the head.

THE TOUCH OF FAITH

It is the touch of faith that can bring about a divine lift from the prison of barrier. You need faith in God. It is only this kind of faith that will enable you to have full realization of your potentials. The Bible says;

Hebrews 11:6: But without faith it is impossible to please him: for he that cometh to God must believe that he is, and that he is a rewarder of them that diligently seek him.

The story of the woman with the issue of blood illustrates what it really means to exercise faith.in God. At the time the woman got her miracle, many people had touched the garment of Jesus without faith. And this made them not to be able to get anything from Him. In fact, so many people have even touched Jesus himself without faith and they remained in their former states.

When you have faith in God, all things will change for the best. Unbelief will keep you under the bondage of the devil. And this is what has made so many to look for miracles without getting it. It is obvious that there is a need for you to depend upon God before your barriers can give way to groundbreaking breakthroughs.

Mark 5:25-34: And a certain woman, which had an issue of

PRAYING AGAINST THE SPIRIT OF THE VALLEY

blood twelve years, And had suffered many things of many physicians, and had spent all that she had, and was nothing bettered, but rather grew worse, When she had heard of Jesus, came in the press behind, and touched his garment. For she said, If I may touch but his clothes, I shall be whole. And straightway the fountain of her blood was dried up; and she felt in her body that she was healed of that plague. And Jesus, immediately knowing in himself that virtue had gone out of him, turned him about in the press, and said, Who touched my clothes? And his disciples said unto him, Thou seest the multitude thronging thee, and sayest thou, Who touched me? And he looked round about to see her that had done this thing. But the woman fearing and trembling, knowing what was done in her, came and fell down before him, and told him all the truth. And he said unto her, Daughter, thy faith hath made thee whole; go in peace, and be whole of thy plague.

THE POWER OF FAITH

Faith is a major prerequisite for having God's blessings upon your life. If this woman had not exercised faith, she would have remained in her problem for the rest of her life. Although there were barriers on her way, she pressed towards where she could lay hands on the garment of Jesus. Getting there she exercised faith and touched the helm of his garment. This action brought her deliverance from a long-standing yoke of the devil. You can also touch the helm of the garment of Jesus by faith today.

THE ROAD IS NOT SMOOTH

The road to anything good in life is never easy. In other words, the road to every good thing in life has barriers. If you need a good husband or wife, there would be a barrier. Getting wholesome in the spirit and in the body is not an easy thing. If you want God's promotion, elevation and breakthrough, you must expect barriers. You will definitely face a barrier if you want to have breakthroughs and leap over your walls of Jericho.

THE HORRIBLE BARRIER

There are different kinds of barriers. Barriers can come in the area of health, business, academics and spiritual life. But the most horrible is a spiritual barrier. This affects every other areas of life. When you are not spiritually balanced, you will have problems with other areas of life. That is why your spiritual life must be given prominent attention so that other areas will not suffer.

PRAYING AGAINST THE SPIRIT OF THE VALLEY

THE POWER OF DISCERNMENT

One of the ways of overcoming your barrier is to identify it. When you identify the barrier, you have conquered a great battle. This is the first step that will land you safely on the shores of breakthroughs.

There is a philosophy of life, which I want to lay bare before you. You do not see things as they are. You only see things based on the way you are. That means that there are things you might see which could make you panic. While somebody else will see such things and become happy. This shows that the way you see things may be a very terrible barrier or not on your way to victory.

Likewise, the great mountain in your own eyes might be the stumbling block to victory in someone else's. There are some people who easily give up their faith and trust in God after a nightmare. Surrendering yourself to the operation of the devil is a big barrier to your breakthroughs. Therefore, the way you see things would or may be a very terrible barrier to unlocking doors of divine breakthroughs in your life.

OPENED EYES

It is only when your eyes are opened that you can have a fulfilled destiny. You need to pray that God should open the eyes of your mind so you can discover what God has in stock for you. By the time you come up with a clear vision of your destiny, there would be less struggling. You will be focussed in life and ministry when your eyes are opened to see the glorious destiny ahead of you.

TOUCH GOD, SO THAT YOU CAN BE TOUCHED

The secret of receiving a touch from God is to touch Him. The woman with the issue of blood touched Jesus Christ and this brought about the touch of heaven upon her soul. When you touch God, He will touch you. It is when you touch God that things will turn for better in your life. Just a touch of God can lead to a complete change in your life.

Men and women who have turned the world upside down have been able to do so because they have at one time or the other touched God. It is the touch of God upon your life that brings about total revolution in all the areas of your life.

PRAYING AGAINST THE SPIRIT OF THE VALLEY

God can move into your life and you can also move into the presence and power of God. However, the movement of God into your life is supposed to be a personal decision. How can God move into you becomes the question that demands an urgent answer? God can move into you when you surrender yourself to Jesus as your Lord and Saviour. It is through this experience that God can move into you.

EVERY PROBLEM HAS A MASTER

I want you to understand this fact. Every problem has a master. Also, every problem has an expiry date. Immediately the master of the problem appears, such will give way to the authority and command of the problem solver or the Master. The woman with the issue of blood has been suffering untold financial and health problems. She had gone to many medical centres in a bid to seeking a lasting solution to her problem. But, all her efforts proved abortive. One glorious day, she had the opportunity of meeting the master of the problem and this brought about instantaneous solution. When your problems collide with the power of God, there is bound to be a solution. Pray this prayer fervently.

My problem, hear the word of the Lord, the master has come, in the name of Jesus.

Another fact that I want you to understand is that it is not what the enemy has taken away from you that matters, but what you do with what you have left. The enemy took away all what the woman had, but they could not take away her faith. Faith is the last bus stop that all problems must surrender to the authority and lordship of Jesus.

I want you to understand something as you are reading this book. Although it is possible for the enemy to take away everything from you, it is not possible for him to take unwavering faith. This is so because if your faith had been taken away you would not be able to exercise faith in reading this book.

THE SECRET

The secret of overcoming the problems of life and the barriers, which the devil has placed on your way is this: NEVER GIVE UP. Don't ever surrender to the devil. The woman with the issue of blood would have died in her problem if she had decided to surrender to defeat. This

PRAYING AGAINST THE SPIRIT OF THE VALLEY

woman looked for the Master of the problem and this gave her victory over the deplorable situation.

When you diligently seek the face of the Master, be sure of triumph. The Bible says; Call unto me, and I will answer thee, and shew thee great and mighty things, which thou knowest not. Jer 33:3.

At this juncture, I want you to understand that your destiny can change within a twinkling of an eye. There is no situation or circumstance that can defy the power of God. God has worked in marvellous ways in the past and He has not changed.

You may ask me, "How can I break the barriers to my breakthroughs?" What you need to do is to simply have faith in God. It is faith in God that can give you the desire of your heart. Absolute faith and trust in the power of God will land you at the hall of breakthroughs. Never doubt or waver about the promises of God. The one who has promised you will come to your rescue.

There are many prayer warriors who have no faith. It is only faith that can bring down the blessings of God upon your life and even deliver you from the hands of the enemy.

It is your faith that can break down every barrier between where you are and your desired point.

BARRIER TO BREAKTHROUGHS

At this point, I want to give you some strategies used by the devil to bring about stumbling blocks or barriers in the lives of people who desire breakthroughs. Follow through some of the points listed below and I believe that your life will never remain the same.

☞ PRIDE OF ASSOCIATION

God does not bless the proud. It is upon the broken and lowly people that He usually showers His blessings. God will always resist the proud, but he gives grace to the humble. The Bible says;

1 Peter 5:5-6: Likewise, ye younger, submit yourselves unto the elder. Yea, all of you be subject one to another, and be clothed with humility: for God resisteth the proud, and giveth grace to the humble. Humble yourselves therefore under the mighty hand of God, that he may exalt you in due time:

The woman with the issue of blood would never have received anything if she had given herself to pride. There are some people who look at the structure of the church before

PRAYING AGAINST THE SPIRIT OF THE VALLEY

attending it. Among the people that moved with Jesus were many illiterates and fishermen. The cream of the society did not move with Jesus. That amounted to why Nicodemus could not come to Jesus in the glare of the public. He had to come to Jesus privately in the night.

John 3:1-2: There was a man of the Pharisees, named Nicodemus, a ruler of the Jews: The same came to Jesus by night, and said unto him, Rabbi, we know that thou art a teacher come from God: for no man can do these miracles that thou doest, except God be with him.

☞ FRUSTRATION

Frustration is a major tool used by the devil to bring about a barrier in the lives of those who are desperate for breakthroughs and miracles. A frustrated person is one who has given up to discouragement and doubt. When you become frustrated, you might not be able to get your desired breakthroughs.

The woman with the issue of blood had tried everything but nothing worked out for her. She had spent all her fortunes on drugs, but there seemed to be no improvement. Never give up. The Lord will come and rescue you. The night may look gloomy, but joy comes in the morning.

☞ DISCOURAGEMENT

Discouragement and frustration go hand in hand. It is discouragement that weighs the heart down. A discouraged person is a burdened person Discouragement must be taken out of the way for you to have a lasting breakthrough. Don't get easily discouraged. Persevere and be persistent in your trust in God. It is very easy and possible for the woman with the issue of blood to get discouraged because of her previous encounters with doctors who could not offer her a solution to her problems.

☞ WEAKNESS

It is through weakness that one can lose sight of God's promises and word. You need to gather enough courage to face your problem even when you are weak. Giving into weakness will not give you the desired miracle. Get up from the bed of weakness because your God is still alive. He can heal and he will heal you. Let the weak say I am strong.

☞ PROCRASTINATION

This is another potent weapon that has hindered the blessings of so many people. Do not procrastinate your days of healing and deliverance. This is the set time. God is by

PRAYING AGAINST THE SPIRIT OF THE VALLEY

your side to answer you. If it will take you to spend time to pray and fast, don't put it off till some other convenient time. Go down on your knee and break the barrier of procrastination which can render you impotent.

☞ UNBELIEF

Unbelief is at a variance with faith. When you do not have faith in God, what you are likely to have is unbelief. It is through faith you can overcome the struggles of life. You need faith not unbelief if you really desire a miracle.

James 1:5-9: If any of you lack wisdom, let him ask of God, that giveth to all men liberally, and upbraideth not; and it shall be given him. But let him ask in faith, nothing wavering. For he that wavereth is like a wave of the sea driven with the wind and tossed. For let not that man think that he shall receive any thing of the Lord. A double minded man is unstable in all his ways. Let the brother of low degree rejoice in that he is exalted:

Unbelief and doubt are not from God. They are barriers to God's blessings. That is why you need to clear away such a thing from you in order to receive God's best for your life. Impossibility is not found in God. It is what exists in the realm of the mortals. Things will begin to change for better when you have faith in God's promises.

☞ AUTHORITY WITHOUT POWER

I read a thrilling story about General Napoleon. There was a time he wanted to inspect the soldiers who were on line. At that time, he was on a horse while the other soldiers were standing at alert for him to inspect them. Suddenly, the horse became furious. It wanted to throw off the General. The soldiers were just looking at him because they were obliged to stand at alert. As this continued, a recruit came out from the midst of the crowd of soldiers, standing at alert and struggled to calm the raging horse. He actually did.

After doing this, General Napoleon instantaneously declared him a captain, but none of the other soldiers recognized him as a captain because he had not been decorated with the rank officially. This soldier decided to go back to General Napoleon and told him that the other soldiers did not recognize him as a captain. The reply of Napoleon was that he should go out and act as a captain. After doing this, he should then come back to him if the other soldiers would not recognize him as one.

With that challenge, the recruit-turn captain got out and shouted a command to a fellow soldier to stop. Surprisingly, the soldier stopped. This made him to continue as a captain

PRAYING AGAINST THE SPIRIT OF THE VALLEY

issuing commands all over the barracks with people respecting him. As time progressed, other soldiers started calling him captain.

You may die in the position which satan has put you if you don't rise to the challenge of confronting the devil. You have the wherewithal to command the devil and all the hosts of hell to stand at alert but it is only faith that will see you through.

☞ THE NAME OF JESUS

A woman had a mad daughter. This daughter had to be taken to a psychiatric hospital for proper treatment. The insanity of the daughter was so serious that her problem aggravated anytime she heard or saw any of her family members. This made the hospital to inform her family members not to pay her any visit..

But, the girl's mother decided to take a step of faith to see her. On getting there, she was advised not to see her daughter because her problem might get worse. The woman despised the report of the daughter and believed the report of God.

Isaiah 53:1: Who hath believed our report? and to whom is the arm of the Lord revealed?

Immediately the woman entered where the mad daughter was kept, the girl wanted to attack her. At that point the mother raised her hands and said, "I command that spirit to depart from you in the name of Jesus." Suddenly, the face of this daughter changed and she began to ask her mother what they were doing there. The woman was flabbergasted. The doctors had to come around because it was the mother that was shouting now and not the daughter. When the doctors got there, they saw what had happened and this woman shouting, "I have power, I know that I have God's power in me."

☞ THE GREATEST BARRIER

At this juncture, I want you to know that the greatest barrier you can ever have is the barrier of sin. Sin is dangerous. It can hinder your prayer from getting to God. Salvation from sin will help you to live a life of dominion. Call upon the name of God so that this barrier may be taken out of your way before praying the prayer points below.

PRAYING AGAINST THE SPIRIT OF THE VALLEY

PRAYER POINTS

1. Oh God, be God in my situation in the name of Jesus.

2. Every barrier on my way to breakthroughs, die in the name of Jesus.

3. Holy Ghost fire, bulldoze my way to breakthroughs in the name of Jesus.

4. Inherited Red Sea blocking my ways to the promised land, divide in the name of Jesus.

5. Every spiritual barrier hanging over my head, scatter in the name of Jesus.

Other Publications by Dr. D. K. Olukoya

1. Be Prepared
2. Breakthrough Prayers For Business Professionals
3. Brokenness
4. Born Great, But Tied Down
5. Can God Trust You?
6. Criminals In The House of God
7. Contending For The Kingdom
8. Dealing With Local Satanic Technology
9. Dealing With Witchcraft Barbers
10. Dealing With Hidden Curses
11. Dealing With The Evil Powers of Your Father's House
12. Dealing With Unprofitable Roots
13. Deliverance: God's Medicine Bottle
14. Deliverance By Fire
15. Deliverance From Spirit Husband And Spirit Wife
16. Deliverance of The Conscience
17. Deliverance of The Head
18. Destiny Clinic
19. Drawers of Power From The Heavenlies
20. Dominion Prosperity
21. Evil Appetite
22. Facing Both Ways
23. Fasting And Prayer
24. Failure In The School Of Prayer
25. For We Wrestle . . .
26. Holy Cry

Other Publications by Dr. D. K. Olukoya

27. Holy Fever
28. How To Obtain Personal Deliverance (Second Edition)
29. Idols Of The Heart
30. Is This What They Died For?
31. Limiting God
32. Meat For Champions
33. Overpowering Witchcraft
34. Personal Spiritual Check-up
35. Power Against Coffin Spirits
36. Power Against Destiny Quenchers
37. Power Against Dream Criminals
38. Power Against Local Wickedness
39. Power Against Marine Spirits
40. Power Against Spiritual Terrorists
41. Power Must Change Hands
42. Pray Your Way To Breakthroughs (Third Edition)
43. Prayer Rain
44. Prayer Strategies For Spinsters And Bachelors
45. Prayer Warfare Against 70 Mad Spirits
46. Prayers To Destroy Diseases And Infirmities
47. Prayers To Move From Minimum To Maximum
48. Praying Against The Spirit of The Valley
49. Praying To Dismantle Witchcraft
50. Release From Destructive Covenants
51. Revoking Evil Decrees
52. Satanic Diversion Of The Black Race

Other Publications by Dr. D. K. Olukoya

53. Silencing The Birds of Darkness
54. Smite The Enemy And He Will Flee
55. Spiritual Warfare And The Home
56. Strategic Praying
57. Strategy Of Warfare Praying
58. Students In The School Of Fear
59. The Enemy Has Done This
60. The Evil Cry of Your Family Idol
61. The Fire Of Revival
62. The Great Deliverance
63. The Internal Stumbling Block
64. The Lord Is A Man Of War
65. The Prayer Eagle
66. The Pursuit of Success
67. The Star In Your Sky
68. The Secrets of Greatness
69. The Serpentine Enemies
70. The Slow Learners
71. The Snake in The Power House
72. The Spirit Of The Crab
73. The Tongue Trap
74. The Way of Divine Encounter
75. The Wealth Transfer Agenda
76. The Vagabond Spirit
77. Unprofitable Foundations
78. Victory Over Satanic Dreams (Second Edition)

Other Publications by Dr. D. K. Olukoya

79. Violent Prayers Against Stubborn Situations
80. War At The Edge of Breakthroughs
81. When God Is Silent
82. Wealth Must Change Hands
83. When You Are Knocked Down
84. Woman! Thou Art Loosed.
85. Your Battle and Your Strategy
86. Your Foundation and Destiny
87. Your Mouth and Your Deliverance
88. Adura Agbayori (Yoruba Version of the Second Edition of Pray Your Way to Breakthroughs)
89. Awon Adura Ti Nsi Oke Nidi (Yoruba Prayer Book)
90. Pluie de Prières
91. Esprit Vagabondage
92. En Finir avec les Forces Maléfiques de la maison de Ton Père
93. Que l'envoûtement perisse
94. Frappez l'adversaire et il fuira
95. Comment recevoir la délivrance du Mari et de la Femme de Nuit
96. Comment se delvrer soi-même
97. Pouvoir Contre les Terroristes Spirituels
98. Prières de Percées pour les hommes d'affaires
99. Prier Jusqu'à Remporter la Victoire
100. Prières Violentes pour humilier les problèmes opiniâtres
101. Le Combat Spirituel et le Foyer
102. Bilan Spirituel Personnel
103. Victoire sur les Rêves Sataniques
104. Prayers That Bring Miracles

Other Publications by Dr. D. K. Olukoya

105. Let God Answer By Fire
106. Prayers To Mount With Wings As Eagles
107. Prayers That Bring Explosive Increase
108. Prayers For Open Heavens
109. Prayers To Make You Fulfill Your Divine Destiny
110. Prayers That Make God To Answer and Fight By Fire
111. Prayers That Bring Unchallengeable Victory and Breakthrough Rainfall Bombardments

BOOK ORDER

Is there any book written by **Dr. D.K Olukoya** (General Overseer MFM Ministries) that you would like to have:

Have you seen his latest books?
To place order for this end time materials.

Text your request as follows:
- Book Title(s)
- Name:
- Delivery Address:
- Text to: 08161229775

Battle cry ministries... equipping the saints of God

God bless you.

Praying Against The Spirit of The Valley

Many spend their entire lifetime traversing the landscape of the valley. Unknown to multitudes, the devil has programmed the majority to the tail region.

The mystery of the spirit of the valley is exposed. This book offers a lifetime opportunity to everyone who wants to come out of the valley and move to the mountain top. This book is a must read. It is readable, rewarding and didactic.

About the Author

Dr. D. K. Olukoya is the General Overseer of the Mountain of Fire and Miracles Ministries and The Battle Cry Christian Ministries.

The Mountain of Fire and Miracles Ministries' Headquarters is the largest single Christian congregation in Africa with attendance of over 120,000 in single meetings.

MFM is a full gospel ministry devoted to the revival of Apostolic signs, Holy Ghost Fireworks, miracles and the unlimited demonstration of the power of God to deliver to the uttermost. Absolute holiness within and without as spiritual insecticide and prerequisite for heaven is openly taught. MFM is a do-it-yourself Gospel Ministry, where your hands are trained to wage war and your fingers to do battle.

Dr. Olukoya holds a first class honours degree in Micro-biology from the University of Lagos and a PhD in Molecular Genetics from the University of Reading, United Kingdom. As a researcher, he has over seventy scientific publications to his credit.

Anointed by God, Dr. Olukoya is a prophet, evangelist, teacher and preacher of the Word. His life and that of his wife, Shade and their son Elijah Toluwani are living proofs that all power belongs to God.

ISBN - 978-38083-5-4

www.ingramcontent.com/pod-product-compliance
Lightning Source LLC
Chambersburg PA
CBHW060857050426
42453CB00008B/992